leapfrog Learners

# Pirates

## by Annabelle Lynch

# W
# FRANKLIN WATTS

First published in 2012 by
Franklin Watts
338 Euston Road
London
NW1 3BH

Franklin Watts Australia
Level 17/207 Kent Street
Sydney
NSW 2000

Picture credits: Shutterstock: front cover bg, 5, 6-7;
itsockphoto - front cover, 10, 12, 16; Alamy 15;
Wikipedia Commons 4, 18.; Corbis 20-21.

A CIP catalogue record for this book is
available from the British Library.

Dewey number: 910.4'5-dc23

ISBN 978 1 4451 0320 4 (hbk)
ISBN 978 1 4451 0328 0 (pbk)

Series Editor: Melanie Palmer
Picture Researcher: Diana Morris
Series Advisor: Catherine Glavina
Series Designer: Peter Scoulding

Printed in China

Franklin Watts is a division of Hachette Children's Books,
an Hachette UK company. www.hachette.co.uk

# Contents

The words in **bold** can be found in the glossary.

# What are pirates?

Pirates are **thieves** who live at sea. They attack ships to rob them of their **goods**.

In the past, pirates often wore hats and jewellery.

# Pirate ships

Long ago, pirates sailed in tall ships. They chased the other ships on the sea!

Pirate ships were much faster than other ships.

# Life on board

Pirates spent a lot of time on board their ships. They often fought with each other!

Pirates drank a lot of rum!

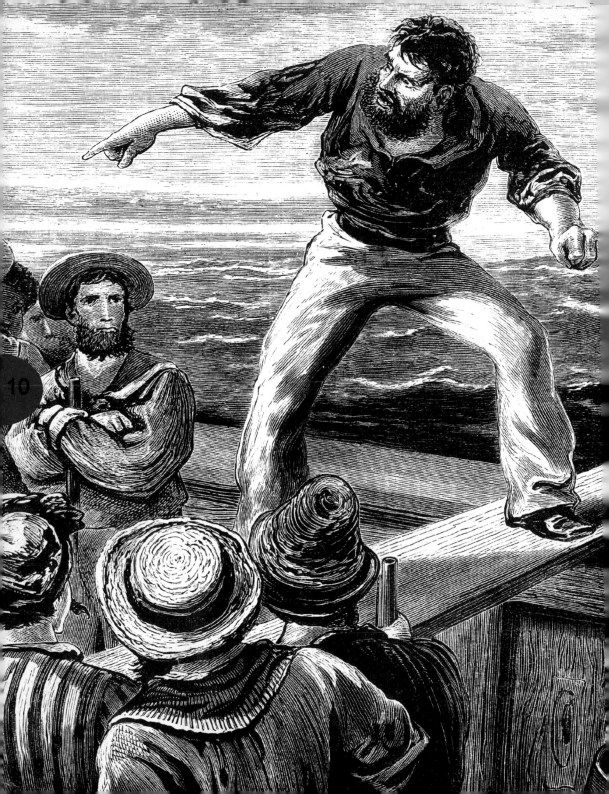

# Punishment

If a pirate was bad, the **punishment** was too. Sometimes they had to 'walk the plank'.

If you walked the plank, you fell into the sea and could drown!

# pirate flags

Pirate ships flew
a special flag.
This warned other
ships to **surrender**
or risk an attack.

The pirate flag is called
the Jolly Roger.

# Into battle!

Pirates loved battles! They used swords, guns, and **cannons** to fight other ships.

This pirate ship has caught fire in battle!

# Buried treasure

Pirates buried their
stolen treasure on
desert islands.
They hid it from
other pirates!

Pirates drew maps to find
their buried treasure. An X
marked the hiding place.

# Blackbeard

Blackbeard was a pirate with a long, dark beard. He killed many people in battle!

Can you see Blackbeard in this picture?

# Pirates today

Some pirates still sail the seas today. They look for big ships to steal things from.

Modern pirates use speed boats to chase ships.

# Glossary

**Cannons** - type of gun that fires heavy metal balls

**Goods** - objects that are useful such as food

**Thieves** - people who take things that do not belong to them

**Punishment** - what you have to do if you have done something wrong

**Surrender** - to give up in a battle

## Websites:

http://www.nationalgeographic.com/pirates

http://www.talklikeapirate.com

http://www.thekidswindow.co.uk/News/Pirates.htm

Every effort has been made by the Publishers to ensure that the websites are suitable for children, and that they contain no inappropriate or offensive material. However, because of the nature of the Internet, it is impossible to guarantee that the contents of these sites will not be altered. We strongly advise that Internet access is supervised by a responsible adult.

# Quiz

1.  Where do pirates live?

2.  What did pirates do with their treasure?

3.  What happened if a pirate was bad?

4.  What is the name of the pirate flag?

5.  How do modern pirates travel?

6.  Which famous pirate had a long beard?

The answers are on page 24

# Answers

1. At sea
2. Buried it on a desert island
3. They had to walk the plank
4. The Jolly Roger
5. On speed boats
6. Blackbeard

# Index